The Invitation

Mary Allen

Copyright © 2017 Mary Allen

Farrand Avenue Faith Publishing

ISBN - 13: 978-0-9887841-3-0
ISBN-10: 0988784130

Water color illustrations by Susan Thompson
All rights reserved.

I dedicate this book to my grandchildren Claudia, Caitlyn, and John (Hunter), who have been instrumental in driving home the point Jesus makes about putting God first above what and whom we love dearly.

Also, to my foster and adopted grandchildren: Elizabeth Faith, Cheyanne, Indigo, Gabe, Justin, Julius, A.J. and the others who have come, stayed for a bit and moved. You are living proof of the great riches that giving all to God reaps. What a surprising impact all of you have made on me!

Each one of my "Grands" is a blessing beyond measure.

The Invitation

After hearing him teach, the rich young ruler fell to his knees. "Jesus, you are perfectly good!"

Jesus answered, "God only is perfectly good. Do you accept that I AM?"

The rich man nodded he would. He said, "Jesus, I've watched little children be blessed by you. If such enter heaven, what should I do? I'm no longer a child, but I have obeyed every law, each command from little boy days.

"If the innocent are assured of their places in glory, shouldn't I have the same end to my life's story? Jesus, if only I knew, I'd certainly do whatever it takes to secure heaven's treasure. Please, tell me how, the precise weight or measure."

Jesus saw into the man's heart. He knew the man thought his words were true, but that he really loved his money most and all the things that it could do. "You have done well on your own, but it isn't enough. Come follow me. Sell all your stuff. Give it away to benefit the poor. Put God first to gain heaven's rich store."

Shaking his head, the man rose to explain how his position, his wealth, and yes, even his family's good name must be preserved. It was his duty. It was his job. He'd keep God's commands, he would feed the poor mob, but he wouldn't – he couldn't – sell all that he had to just follow Jesus. He turned away sad.

Jesus said, "It's harder for the rich to enter the kingdom of God, than a camel to push through a slit in a rod. They find it harder to surrender without bargain or wheedle than for coarse camel hair to thread a fine needle."

We disciples were shocked and said to each other, "Who then can get in? Who'd chance to bother? Aren't riches promised to those who don't waver? Doesn't Jehovah bestow wealth on those who find favor?" Puzzled, we finally worked up nerve to ask.

Jesus replied, "The first commandment is to put nothing before God. Some people try to buy heaven on their terms, with a wink and a nod. Those who keep in first place the things they love or desire will lose all, and themselves, in an eternal fire.

"Come, all. Make me first in your heart; God alone serve and adore. Get rid of anything else that you might love more. You'll gain riches in heaven, far beyond measure, endlessly vast. In short, God places the meek of heart over all. Those grasping for first shall be last."

ABOUT THE AUTHOR

Mary Allen lives in Northwest Indiana with her family and a German Wire-haired Pointer named Jake. She loves words and wordplay, but not as much as she loves Jesus. She has authored three books of poetry and was named La Porte County Poet Laureate 2010-11. "The Invitation" is adapted from one of her poems. Allen loves to write women's fiction and published the first of her works, "God's Love Most Gentle", in 2015.

ABOUT THE ILLUSTRATOR

Susan Thompson is a grateful follower of Jesus, and a wife, mother of three grown sons and an ever-learning artist. She lives on a small farm in northwest Indiana complete with a windmill and pond. Her favorite painting is the "Song of the Lark" which depicts what she knows to be the thrill and awe of the simple and beautiful moments available to all of us in this miraculous world in which we live. Her favorite book of the Bible is James packed full of wisdom about how earthly life is like a vanishing vapor. That truth compels her to live each day and moment to the fullest. God is good!

WHAT I REALLY MEAN IS…

Besides sharing this true story of Jesus, I also like to introduce children to words they may not be familiar with or words they have heard, but have a fuzzy idea of what they mean. Below I've listed some words and phrases that I've used in this book. I hope this helps children fully understand what the story means.

A wink and a nod—this phrase implies unspoken agreement between two parties. It carries the idea of getting around the rules.

Bestow—to give or present an honor, right, or gift.

Meek—today people often think this means weak, but that's not what Jesus meant. When Jesus spoke the word "praus" or "meek" it meant teachable, patient while suffering, not thinking of yourself as better than others, seeing yourself as God sees you – with strengths and faults yet needing Him, just as Jesus was dependent on Father God to do what He did.

Preserve—maintaining, keeping something safe

Wheedle—to coax or persuade someone; to try to get another to come around to your way of thinking.

SOMETHING EXTRA FOR ADULTS

Material wealth can be a tremendous blessing. It can afford a measure of security, pleasure, and opportunity. God blessed many godly people, such as Abraham, with wealth. When this blessing grew so great that the flocks and herds he and his nephew owned could no longer share the same pasturelands, Abraham depended on God to provide and allowed Lot to pick the choicest of the land.

King David took Bathsheba, another man's wife, and sinned with her. God told David that he would have given him many more blessings than being king, but could not excuse this sin. David repented and God blessed him again, but there were consequences David had to pay for his actions.

God also blessed Solomon. First with the wisdom he asked to have to be a great ruler, and then with unimaginable wealth besides. However, in his later years, Solomon unwisely wed heathen women to expand his wealth on his own. He allowed his heart to turn from trust in God. It was his undoing.

Therefore we see that it's not the riches God has a problem with, but rather how people use it. Some people are poor. They have nothing or very little and still they are so consumed with desire for and the love of money that they don't trust God either. God cares whether the love of money, power, prestige become more important than God himself.

God created the world and owns everything. Riches don't tempt God, but riches often tempt humans and lead them astray. This was the case with the rich, young ruler. He refused to give up control of his blessings. He saw himself as the owner rather than the steward of the blessings God allowed.

Remember, Abraham would have given up all his wealth to save his son. Isaac was that important to him. When God asked Abraham to give up Isaac, whom he loved greatly, Abraham did. God gave Isaac back to Abraham.

Who knows? If he'd only given it all and put Jesus first, God may have multiplied the rich young ruler's material wealth so that he could do great and wonderful things in God's Kingdom. If God didn't do that, the immeasurable treasures waiting in heaven would still have made the Rich Young Ruler forget all about the things he once held dear here on earth.

It's the same for us whether the path is rough or easy. Make Jesus your forever treasure.

Made in the USA
Monee, IL
29 June 2020